100 Ideas for Better Patient Relations in Registration, Billing, and Collections

Cheryl Sobun
Editor,
The Health Care Biller
The Medical Office Biller
Aspen Publishers, Inc.
Brookfield, Wisconsin

Aspen Publishers, Inc®
Gaithersburg, Maryland
1997

To order quantity of specialized bulk sales of this report, please call Brian Litz, Account Manager for Professional Sales, Aspen Publishers, Inc., at (301) 417-7592.

Orders: (800) 638-8437
Customer Service: (800) 234-1660

Editorial Resources: Ruth Bloom
ISBN: 0-8342-0909-8
ISBN: 978-0-8342-0909-1

Printed in the United States of America

1 2 3 4 5

Contents

Introduction

Excellent patient relations is at the core of any successful health care facility. Without it, you can't ensure that patients will pay their bills on time and return to your facility the next time they need health care services.

Patient relations goes beyond staffing your facility with top-notch physicians and caring, knowledgeable nurses. Every encounter a patient has with the business office and the admitting department staff must also be a pleasant experience. In this day and age of increased deductibles and co-payments, health care business office personnel deal with the public more than ever before.

Excellent patient relations, therefore, begins in the admitting department or registration area, continues in the billing department, and completes the cycle in the collections department.

This report will help you develop good public relations policies and procedures for top-quality customer relations in the admitting, billing, and collections departments. We've highlighted 100 key tips for improving patient relations in these areas, but as you read through this report, you'll probably find hundreds more!

Pointers

No matter what type or what area of a health care facility you work in, ***there are a few common patient relations problems to avoid:***

1. **Waiting in line.** Whether at a bank, hospital, or amusement park, people hate waiting in lines. When patients wait in line at a hospital or clinic, having too few people helping them, it only adds fuel to the fire.
   Solution: Make certain your registration, cashier, and customer service areas are well-staffed. This is especially important during peak hours. For physician offices: Try to call scheduled patients if the doctor is running behind.
2. **Voice mail and answering machines.** When people call your facility, they usually want to speak to a real, live person. They don't want to listen to a computerized voice telling them to press numbers on the telephone (especially if they have a rotary phone)!
   Solution: Always try to have people answering telephones and taking messages.

3. **Poorly-trained employees.** It's very frustrating for patients to try and find answers when an employee doesn't know how to help them.
   Solution: Train everyone who works with patients on all policies and procedures. Cross-training employees is a good way to make sure your staff knows exactly how the office operates.
4. **Complicated insurance forms.** Patients, like everyone else, become frustrated when they don't understand the forms they need to sign.
   Solution: Even though you can't control the forms used by your patients' insurance companies, you can try to make your own forms a little more user-friendly.
5. **Being told one price and being asked to pay another.** The price people are quoted for anything is what they expect to pay.
   Solution: Make certain your patients realize the price you are quoting them is only an estimate, and that the actual price will probably be different.

Customer Service Quiz

Before you continue with this report, take this brief customer service quiz to find out your own level of customer service skills (Exhibit 1).

Exhibit 1 Customer Service Quiz

Rate yourself on each item, using the following scale:

5—Often
3—Sometimes
1—Rarely
0—Never

1. I try to learn all I can about our department and facility.
2. I try to understand our patients so I can relate to them.
3. If I can't answer a patient's question, I try to get help from someone else.
4. I try to be friendly and courteous to all patients—even those who aren't courteous to me.
5. I respect a patient's need for time to make a decision.
6. I'm willing to work with a patient past my quitting time, if necessary.
7. I always speak highly of our facility.
8. I avoid saying negative things about our policies and procedures.
9. I avoid "chit chatting" with other employees in the presence of patients.
10. I willingly help my fellow employees as necessary.

Total

Scoring:

Total your answers and use the following scale to determine how your patient relations skills rate:

45–50: You are top-notch when it comes to customer service.

30–44: You should go over the quiz again and see where you can profit from personal improvement.

0–29: You'll want to do a lot of soul-searching about your current behavior. Try to make some real changes before your boss has a go at it!

If you scored between 45–50 on the test, then your facility is lucky to have you on board. But maybe your staff could stand improvement. Either way, you can use this report as a self-help guide or as a training manual for your department.

1

The Registration Department: Beyond Service with a Smile

No one will argue that treating patients with kindness and respect is an essential part of a registrar or admitting clerk's job. But there are many other essential ingredients that go into a top-notch public relations recipe.

This chapter will explain:

- How to be friendly, professional, and respectful.
- How to collect self-pay dollars without hurting patient relations.
- How to reduce waiting time and other customer service ideas.
- How to deal with irate patients.
- Why it's important to train the registration staff in the art of patient relations.

HOW TO BE FRIENDLY, PROFESSIONAL, AND RESPECTFUL

1. Kill 'em with kindness.

Have you ever been treated poorly by a bank teller or department store clerk? Everyone has at one time or another. Think back. How did it make you feel? Did you cooperate with that person? Probably not. Tensions were high and you felt stressed. When you finally left the building and the bad situation behind, you probably mumbled "jerk," or a similar word. Chances are you were still upset as you drove home.

If you're like most people, you like a courteous, professional approach in all business transactions. The job of the admitting/registration department is to make patients feel at ease, instantly. The old adage, "Kill 'em with kindness," really works! If you're perfectly friendly and helpful, you'll make even the grumpiest of patients warm up to you.

Here are four ways to accomplish this:

1. **Greeting**—Say hello in a warm, empathetic voice. This indicates your willingness to help. It also inspires the patient's confidence in you. If you glare at patients, look way too busy, and robotically ask for information without taking the time to smile and say hello, then you're off to a bad start. Patients will have a poor first impression of you, and they'll respond in kind.

Note: The terms "admitting" and "registration" will be used interchangeably in this report. It can refer to the admitting or registration department in a hospital, or the registration area in a physician office or clinic.

2. **Listen**—Don't just go through the motions. Listen actively. You'll learn a lot if you put some effort into listening.
3. **Provide/refer/obtain**—Be helpful to the patient. Many times, your patient is unsure of what comes next. It's your job to make the patient feel comfortable.
4. **Conclude**—Thank the patient for being cooperative. Make sure patients understand where to go next or about how long it will be before the doctor will see them.

If you follow these four steps, patients will be friendlier, and you'll get better quality registration information.

Customer Service Checklist

There are as many definitions of good customer service as there are businesses. For example, some of your patients might want friendly registrars who listen carefully and avoid tying up their time. Other patients might want a registrar who is sympathetic to their health situation.

In the end, service is not merely what you do for patients, but how you do it. This provides a reasonable basis for comparison between your facility and every other, regardless of size. In fact, basic patient expectations for service are fairly consistent across the board—and often come down to the simplest of details.

How important is customer service to your patients? It's as important as patients themselves. You may win patients with a discount or special service, but someone is always waiting to undercut your price or deliver a comparable product. The only way to keep customers coming back is through service. And the payoff for relationships based on good service is handsome. Health care facilities with strong reputations for service usually receive more money and have higher profit margins than their competitors.

When you keep customers through good service, you create a positive cycle of higher profit margins, greater rewards for registrars, low employee turnover, better customer service, and higher patient satisfaction. With the cost of hiring each new employee ranging from a few hundred to several thousand dollars, keeping turnover at a minimum is a worthy goal in itself. Similarly, bad service creates a cycle that reduces patient satisfaction over time.

Here are a few points to consider regarding your registration department's level of customer service:

- Do registrars present a pleasant and helpful image?
- Do they ask questions of the patients?
- Do they listen to patients' needs and concerns?
- How well do they respond to patient objections?
- Are they prompt in getting back to the patient on open issues?
- Do they show confidence in the facility's ability to serve the patients' needs?
- Do they give the patient confidence?

2. Make a good first impression.

Registration offers the health care facility many opportunities to score public relations points. On the other hand, any employee who deals with the public has the opportunity to upset or alienate a patient. Make a good impression, and the registration process will flow with ease. Patients will feel comfortable giving you information, confident that they're dealing with a professional. A bad impression makes patients leery of your ability.

How do you make a good first impression? ***To better the chance of a positive patient encounter, the following customer relations principles should be incorporated into all contacts with patients:***

Avoid Terms of Endearment—Call patients by their last name using Mr., Mrs., Ms. as a sign of respect.

Communicate Effectively—Be natural. Use words patients can understand. Be careful of technical jargon that may be unfamiliar to patients.

Use a Pleasant Tone of Voice—Greet patients in firm, well-modulated tones. Avoid sounding shrill, loud, or hesitant. Instead, aim to speak in a pleasing, assertive manner. How you sound often says more than your actual words. If there's a discrepancy between your words and the sound of your voice, people believe the sound of your voice.

Look Professional—Adhere to dress codes. Look neat and clean. How you dress often affects how you behave. Dress for success. It will help you register patients with confidence and authority.

Act Professionally—Avoid slang. Never yell or make a scene in front of a patient or in a patient contact area.

Use Nonverbal Communication—Maintain eye contact. Watch your posture and facial expressions. Stand tall. Sit up straight. Use open gestures when working with patients. Slouch in your chair, and you send a message to patients that you're not interested in them or in what you're doing. Body language accounts for 55 percent of your believability, according to Carol Schneider-Jenkins, a communication and image specialist. Sit facing patients when collecting registration information. Use well-balanced, relaxed motions. Avoid a stiff, rigid posture. Be assured and strong, yet warm.

Smile Pleasantly—Try to smile as often as possible, without appearing insincere. A smile helps establish a rapport and tells patients you are interested in helping them. Like the tone of your voice, sometimes your face speaks louder than your words.

Be Perceptive—Anticipate the patient's needs and respond. Be aware of common questions and concerns of patients and cater to them.

Handle Complaints Gracefully—Don't become part of the problem. Let patients calm down and address their concerns immediately.

Respect the Patient's Dignity—All patients deserve your respect. Never say or do anything that may embarrass the patient.

Be Patient—Many of your patients are elderly or sick. Consider how you would want to be treated if you were in their place.

HOW TO COLLECT SELF-PAY DOLLARS WITHOUT HURTING PATIENT RELATIONS

Health care facilities are finding out that the old policy of letting patients waltz in, receive services, and waltz out without paying a dime is becoming passé.

Patients in the 1990s have more out-of-pocket health care expenses than ever before. Health care services are more expensive than ever before. And it's a fact: As soon as patients walk out the door, your bill gets put on the bottom of their priority list. They're on the road to recovery now, and things like rent, utilities, and credit card bills take precedence.

But there's an uproar heard from registrars across the country—"How can we maintain good patient relations while taking bus fare from little old ladies?"

3. Be courteous when making patients aware that payment is expected.

There are several ways to get the message across to patients that you expect to be paid at the time of service. ***It can be stated in four ways:***

1. **When a patient makes an appointment.** When a patient calls for an appointment, the person scheduling the patient can inform him or her that any co-payments will be expected at the time of service. Or, the scheduler may say, *"The office visit will be about $________. And for your convenience, we accept cash, checks, and credit cards."*
2. **When a patient registers or checks out.** Possible phrases are, *"That will be a $10 co-pay for today." "The office visit comes to $________. Would you like to pay for that by cash, check, or credit card?"* or *"I see your*

insurance pays 80 percent, and you've met your deductible. Your portion of the bill comes to $________."

3. **Visually with a sign on the front desk or in a brochure.** Clearly stating your payment policy on a sign or in a brochure backs you up and gets the message across to everyone.
4. **Any or all of the above used in conjunction.**

The tips above for collecting payment up front are all well and good, but they'll backfire if you don't pay attention to good patient relations. **Treating the patient courteously is key!** If the patient responds to your request for payment with, *"I didn't know I had to pay. I didn't bring any money with me,"* don't snap back, *"Well, that's our policy. I'm only doing my job."* You'll kill any chance for good patient relations with that remark. Be understanding of the patient's dilemma. Say, *"I understand. We can bill you for your portion this time. But please bring your co-payment with you next time. Here's a brochure that tells you all about our practice and our payment policy."* With this statement, you've smoothed things over. The patient will leave in a good mood. You've just increased the chances that the patient will pay when he or she receives the bill and will bring the co-payment next time. **Remember:** Registration without favorable public relations will lead to the demise of the person responsible, and will collect fewer dollars in the long run. Building a registration system consistent with good public relations is critical to the success of your registration program and strategy.

A good registrar is:

- a good communicator
- a good listener
- tolerant and patient
- a good organizer
- prompt in dealing with the patient by telephone or in person

Registrars who have not mastered public relations skills, or do not give them proper emphasis, eventually move on to other fields—by request or otherwise.

How Policies and Procedures Come into Play

Maintaining favorable public relations while pursuing an active registration and collection program doesn't depend entirely on favorable face-to-face contacts. How effective your registration policies and procedures are also determine favorable or unfavorable public relations. Lack of attention to policies and procedures can cause adverse public relations in the registration process, no matter how good your personal human relations skills or those of your staff.

Registration Policy

Your registration policy should stress maintaining the highest level of patient public relations while protecting the receivables.

4. Develop a registration policy that covers the majority of situations, and have administration review it for approval and backing.

When you don't have a registration policy, you have nothing to fall back on or refer to when a public relations situation comes up. A policy will give you and your staff backing, support, and direction. Develop the registration policy, get it approved, then make sure everyone is trained.

5. Review the existing registration procedures before and after a public relations problem comes up and question whether that procedure should be revised.

Look at your existing procedures and keep this in mind as you develop new ones: "What will this do to our public relations?"

6. Make sure everyone is trained on the policies and procedures.

Train staff in the use of the registration procedures and make sure they're being followed. Let staff members help develop the procedures. That way, they'll be more likely to follow them. Likewise, review policies with staff to be sure they're being followed. See Exhibit 1-1 for solutions for improving patient relations in Admissions and Registration.

Exhibit 1–1 Improving Patient Relations in Admissions and Registration

Public Relations Problems	Recommended Fixes
1. Poor quality of information from all points of patient registration.	a. Monitor information and give feedback on errors, omissions, etc. Insist on quality at all points of registration. b. Stress the importance of getting more information at registration. c. Train the registration staff in collections—why information is required. d. Verify critical information with copies of all identification or insurance cards. e. Develop a good, productive preregistration program.
2. Lack of knowledge of what is done in registration by internal departments.	a. Have meetings with various departments to explain objectives in more detail. b. Have a regular feature in an organization newsletter. c. Have an open house in the business office. d. Communicate more regularly with administration and other department heads. e. Invite other departments to your staff meetings. f. Make presentations at their meetings.
3. Lack of knowledge by the public of what to expect.	a. Do some positive advertising in local newspapers and magazines, and have open houses. b. Conduct educational classes for the public. c. Give written handout material at registration. d. Do a public relations survey by phone after service is rendered to go over charges, bills, collection policy, etc.
4. Poor service by the registration staff.	a. Train staff in technical areas and human relations. b. Upgrade job requirements. c. Pay competitive wages to keep good quality registrars. d. Give the staff incentives and recognition for good performance in public relations. e. Reduce stress in the office and at registration points. f. Have managers give more support to the staff when public relations problems arise with administration.

7. Publish brochures stating these policies and procedures.

As stated earlier, brochures are one way to get the message across to patients that payment is expected at the time of service. Brochures are also your tool for getting any other policies across to patients. At the Chicago office of Dr. Bharat K. Shah, a patient brochure was designed to inform patients about the practice and its policies. The reason for the brochure, says Cheri Bryant, office manager, is because patients often were in the dark about what to expect from their physician and his office staff. The brochure includes everything from where to park, to house calls, to the up-front payment policy. It's worded in an informative and friendly way, not confrontational. For example, the "Fees and Payments" segment reads:

> *We make every effort to keep down the cost of your medical care. You can help by paying upon the completion of each visit. Other arrangements can be made with our office manager, depending upon your special circumstances.*

Bryant says frequent questions from patients prompted them to write the brochure. It made sense, and was easier on the patients. It gave them the information they wanted without having to ask. The brochure also helps patients understand their insurance, which can be a troublesome topic. It states that office staff, when possible, will help patients to receive maximum benefits. Bryant says the brochure is important to patients, and it leads to fewer problems down the line. "If you tell your patients up front what you expect of them, it makes your life easier, and their life easier, too," she says. The brochure was not a costly undertaking. Bryant estimates the cost was "very nominal, probably not even 25 cents a brochure." Dr. Shah's brochure includes:

- a message from the physician
- the address, telephone number, map, and parking areas
- internal medicine facts
- appointments
- emergency care
- telephone calls
- house calls
- prescriptions or refills
- fees and payments
- insurance
- Medicare information
- HMO and PPO information

Providers interested in creating a similar brochure need to include the particulars about their facility. Also, seek input from patients. Ask them what they would like to see in a brochure.

HOW TO REDUCE WAITING TIME AND OTHER CUSTOMER SERVICE IDEAS

The Importance of Preregistration

A patient doesn't appear at your door hoping to get a good seat and read the latest magazines. That person is there for medical care, and a lengthy wait only aggravates the situation.

8. Preregister patients.

A successful preregistration program can eliminate that aggravation. It also can lay the groundwork for a good flow of information that will follow a patient through admission, treatment, discharge, and billing.

9. Ease patients' wait time.

Although systems may vary, the basis for preadmission is universal. It's rooted in patient service and helps provide patients with what they're there for—treatment, not a long wait in a reception area.

At Sinai Samaritan Medical Center in Milwaukee, Wisconsin, a 580-bed hospital, more than 50 percent of all patients are preadmitted, says Diane E. Beier, admitting manager. The other half are emergency or walk-in outpatients.

The admitting staff is alerted to patients who can be preregistered through schedules sent via computer from each department. Insurance verifications, preauthorizations, and other items are handled before the patient arrives. The average wait time at Sinai Samaritan: 4.25 minutes.

At the 711-bed UCLA Medical Center in Los Angeles, California, preregistration means the wait time is virtually nonexistent. The only time a patient may wait is if a bed is not available. Three preregistration systems are in place, and 65 percent of all patients are preregistered, says Myriam Cabello, assistant director of admissions and registration at the medical center.

First is the appointment scheduling system, which works much like the one at Sinai Samaritan.

Second, physician offices fax an appointment list to the hospital. The admitting staff then contacts patients for preregistration.

Third, the hospital issues telephone index cards and telephone stickers for providers to keep handy. They then can tell patients where to call when referring them to UCLA.

Pagers

Despite all your efforts to curb waiting time, some lengthy waits are still inevitable. Offering a pager for patients who are in for a long wait can give them freedom to leave the waiting room.

The 160-bed Arthur G. James Cancer Hospital and Research Institute in Columbus, Ohio, has a pager program. Patients can stroll through the center, visit the Ohio State University campus where the center is located, or stop at the cafeteria. They can even pay a visit to the mall just 15 minutes down the road. The start-up cost for the cancer center was $100 for 20 pagers (a "cheapo" model).

"We have found that issuing pagers to patients who care to go to the cafeteria, shop in our gift shop, or sightsee has been effective," says Keith B. Keplinger, outpatient care center director at the hospital. "They (patients) may be hungry or just tired of sitting and want to see more of the facility than just the four walls of the waiting area," Keplinger says. "In most cases, patients return before being paged, but the pager has given them some freedom from the waiting area without the risk of being missed. What we've gained in goodwill and patient satisfaction was worth the investment."

Meal Tickets

If patients must wait during meal time, registration staff at the 971-bed Tampa General Hospital in Tampa, Florida, offers meal tickets for food and beverages in the hospital cafeteria. In some cases, the admissions and patient registration director, Alex Freeman, goes out himself, greets patients, gets a wheelchair, if needed, and offers a tour of the hospital.

"They're more upset about being in the hospital rather than the waiting," Freeman says. If he and his staff can keep patients well informed—and sometimes distracted—during that wait, time passes quickly with fewer complaints.

Courtesy Calls

The above tips, such as a pager or meal ticket, might work for hospitals and large clinics. But what of small physician offices? ***Best bet:***

10. Call patients ahead of time.

As soon as you see the doctor is getting backed up, start calling patients to tell them the doctor is running late. Ask if they can come in 15 minutes or 30 minutes later, or if they would like to reschedule.

If something comes up on the physician's schedule days prior, call people right away to explain the situation and reschedule.

Of course, you won't be able to get a hold of everyone. Tell patients when they come in that the doctor is running 30 minutes behind, or is at the hospital on an emergency. Offer to reschedule if there is a long wait time. Suggest the patient come back in 30 minutes or an hour if they have errands to run.

Idea: Have free beverages on hand to offer to patients in order to smooth things over. *Remember*, their time is valuable, too.

11. Reexamine your scheduling policy.

Of course, the best way to handle waiting time woes in a physician office or clinic is to improve scheduling. ***Here are six examples:***

1. Determine the average length of time the physician spends with each patient.
2. Calculate the number of daily appointments possible while still maintaining a realistic schedule.
3. Allow sufficient time in the day for emergency appointments.
4. Set aside extra time for a patient's initial visit. This will allow physicians and staff to collect thorough medical histories. Chances for malpractice suits increase if physicians aren't alerted to critical items, such as drug allergies.
5. Alert patients to any delays as soon as they arrive. If the delays are extreme, call patients at home or work to push back the time of their appointments when possible.
6. Track missed or canceled appointments and follow-up. At worst, cancelations or no-shows are signs of dissatisfaction with the physician or previous bills and require immediate attention.

Battling Language Barriers

Nothing can slow things down like encountering a patient who speaks only Polish or Spanish, for example, when you speak only English. In a country that plays host to an array of cultures, it's inevitable that language barriers will crop up. To maintain good patient relations, those barriers must be broken down.

12. Prepare yourself to handle non-English speaking patients.

- **Schedule** more time for non-English speaking patients.
- **Encourage** English-speaking friends or family of non-English speaking patients to accompany them on visits.
- **Be patient.** Show empathy.
- **Acknowledge** cultural differences. With time, patience, and understanding, you can break down cultural barriers.
- **Send** a memo to all staff members to find out who speaks more than one language or who knows sign language.
- **Compile** an interpreter list. This should include employees' shifts, extensions, and even home telephone numbers. The benefit of in-house interpreters: They understand the industry.
- **Solicit** outside interpretation help from universities, community centers, and churches.
- **Create** a centralized interpretation pool among area providers. This would allow all providers to afford access to skilled interpretation.
- **Consider** creating a special day each week for non-English speaking patients if your community has a lot of them.

AT&T Language Line

The AT&T Language Line can break down any communication barriers via the telephone line. It provides 24-hour access to interpreters who speak more than 140 languages.

Three-way conversations are possible, and there are special programs designed for the health care industry. For more information, call (800) 752-6096.

HOW TO DEAL WITH IRATE PATIENTS

In the Emergency Room

Registrars in the emergency room (ER) have their own problems to contend with. The pressure is on for them to keep their cool and remain professional.

A variety of issues complicate the job for ER registrars. ***Consider:***

- Nearly half of all ER patients don't need emergency treatment, according to a General Accounting Office survey. Still, they demand immediate attention.
- ER visits are on the rise for uninsured or underinsured patients. In these cases, the ER often is the primary care provider.
- Tensions run high in emergency situations. Despite the presence of possibly volatile patients, ER personnel—including registrars—must remain calm.

Registrars, particularly those working in a facility in a less-than-desirable neighborhood, can find themselves in potentially dangerous situations when patients are brought in. ER registrars must know how to respond to violence, and its accompanying chaos.

13. Conduct yourself properly and remain calm in the ER.

Here are some tips to help you handle pressures in the ER if you must deal with hostile patients:

- **Keep your cool.** When patients get abusive, resist the urge to fight back. It will only make the situation worse.
- **Stay focused.** You know what you need to do, so focus on getting it done. This will help you keep your cool, too.
- **Be professional.** Treat patients with dignity and respect. Most will follow your courteous example.
- **Cultivate support.** It's important for emergency room registrars to develop a rapport with the people they work with most directly—the emergency room medical staff.
- **Seek training.** It's unsettling to see people in distress, anxious, and upset. An emergency room registrar needs training in how to deal with patients experiencing a range of emotions, what to expect, when to stay out of the line of fire, and when to call for help.

Handling Patient Complaints

Everyone in registration encounters unhappy patients from time to time. They're no fun to deal with, and sometimes you wish they'd go away. How you handle the hostile patient speaks volumes about your facility.

Treat problem patients properly, and you'll get their repeat business—not to mention the referrals they send your way. Brush them off, and you lose both.

14. Treat complaints as a compliment.

Promptly thank the patient for coming forward. Make assurances that you care and explain how feedback helps you make changes to improve the facility's service.

Above all else, keep your composure when complaints start flying. It won't always be easy, but you'll get nowhere by arguing, making excuses, or trying to shift blame. You must take a hostile patient's complaint head-on to maintain your credibility and build repeat business.

Treat your problem patient politely and with respect, no matter how small the complaint. Once the patient is finished, confirm that you understand and make amends. Ask what you can do to keep his or her business. Often, angry patients just want to vent frustration. If that isn't enough, be prepared to deal with the issue on the spot.

What about the patient who refuses to be consoled? Try your best to remain calm and resolve the situation anyway. Don't think it doesn't matter if you lose these patients as customers. They're the ones most likely to tell others to shun your facility.

15. Get to the root of the complaint.

Your business office should solve the patient's immediate problem, then go one step further. Look for the source of the complaint. What or who within your organization caused the patient to get upset?

For the most part, public relations problems are caused by internal deficiencies. ***They generally can be traced back to these five issues:***

1. Inadequate training of staff members.
2. Lack of updated policies or procedures.
3. Data processing system deficiencies.
4. Inadequate communication with patients on what to expect from providers.
5. Lack of communication or training on procedures of other departments.

Improving quality of service is not an easy task and often requires a lot of time on your part. You need to look at each complaint and ask yourself which of these five issues could have caused the complaint. Often, the first answer is just the surface of what's causing poor public relations. You need to look at all the issues affecting patient relations. See how this works with a complaint that was actually received by a health care facility:

Patient complaint:

> *"I had to wait for more than an hour to see the doctor. To make matters worse, I was asked for my insurance information and a copy of my insurance card, after someone had called me at home prior to my appointment to ask the same questions. I don't think things are handled too well at your facility."*

Typical reaction to this complaint: The manager would send a letter of apology. In some cases, the manager may talk to the registrar about how the customer should have been handled. But to really improve patient relations, take a few more steps. ***Ask yourself:***

- What training issues could have caused this complaint? If a patient was upset about how his or her situation was handled, could this mean the registrars don't know how to handle patients? Have they been trained in good customer service skills?
- What procedural issues could have caused this complaint? Obviously, some employees are unsure of the health care facility's policy. Do they have updated policies? Have they been trained on policies and procedures?
- What system issues could have caused this complaint? Could something be done in the system to prevent patients from being asked the same questions twice?
- What communication issues (with patients or between departments) could have caused this complaint? Do we have a procedure for speeding up the registration process? In this case, the root of the complaint could actually be several things. Using the answers you gave to the questions above, set up a plan to improve the quality of your service. Ask yourself: What can I do to prevent hearing this complaint again?

16. Document and take action to resolve a complaint every time a customer makes one.

- **Provide** training on handling complaints and irate customers.
- **Develop** or update policies and procedures.

- **Investigate** system issues that could prevent this complaint.
- **Train** and inform all employees who deal with patients on policies and procedures.
- **Implement** patient complaint forms like the one on page 43 in Chapter 4, "Getting Patient Feedback."

What To Tell Patients Who Balk at Giving Information

Heard this before? *"What's wrong with you? I just gave you that information last week."* How about this one? *"I've been coming here for 10 years and nothing regarding insurance has changed."*

If you look at it from the patient's point of view, you probably would agree. But it's your job to gather accurate and complete information for every visit.

Tip: Don't say, *"Do you still live at XYZ Barney St.?"* Instead, ask, *"What is your address?"* You'll avoid patients just agreeing with you.

17. Avoid asking questions that command just a yes or no answer.

Here's what you can tell patients who don't want to give you their information again: *"For your benefit, we need to update your file. I'm sure you don't want any billing or collection problems. This information should help us avoid them."*

WHY IT'S IMPORTANT TO TRAIN THE REGISTRATION STAFF IN THE ART OF PATIENT RELATIONS

If you're in charge of a registration department, it's important for your staff to understand why patient relations is such an essential part of their jobs and to incorporate good patient relations into their daily routine.

18. Consider a training program on human relations for registration professionals. Look for seminars that include practicing specific techniques to improve how staff responds to patients.

Added bonus: You'll make staff members feel important by sending them to an all-day seminar. If cost is a concern, send one person and have that person hold a "mini seminar" for other staff members. Or, hold a monthly in-house seminar during lunch and provide a catered meal. Go over points made in this report and areas that could stand improvement at your facility.

Another idea: Get registration staff involved in setting patient relations standards themselves and hold them accountable for upholding those standards.

At the 550-bed Mercy Hospital Medical Center in Des Moines, Iowa, a customer service strategy was built into staff evaluations, says Diane Cummings, manager of admissions and outpatient testing.

The strategy identifies what employees need to do to achieve below average, average, or outstanding ratings. The employees themselves created the criteria for each rating.

To receive an outstanding rating, employees must:

- Participate on committees to promote the customer service strategy.
- Assist in updating the strategy, with managerial assistance.
- Partake in updating policies and procedures.
- Develop tools to monitor the effectiveness of the customer service strategy.

The requirements sound impossible to meet if employees are expected to register patients at the same time. But Cummings says she creates time to allow employees to meet their goals. "They have a lot of power," she notes. "The more I give them, the better they understand and take ownership in the department."

Employees Set High Standards

To craft the customer service strategy, Cummings first turned to employees. She asked them each to fill out a survey which included these four key questions:

1. What does customer service mean to you?
2. Who do you view as your customers?
3. What do you perceive customer expectations are and why?
4. How can you enhance customer service?

The Next Step: Incorporate employee suggestions for the customer service strategy as part of their job evaluation.

"With registration being one of the very first departments a patient comes into contact with, our impression on the patient could impact their whole stay," Cummings says.

Because customer service is difficult to measure, Cummings says she and two supervisors also rely on input from peers and others who come in contact with registration staff.

Note: All input from peers and employees from other departments must be measurable so the peer input element of evaluations doesn't turn into a tool for revenge.

Ask Patients for Feedback

To formally measure how you're doing, send patient surveys (prepaid postage) to patients' homes. Or keep patient survey postcards at the registration desk. ***Other ideas:***

- Monitor and respond to complaints.
- Let patients know you want to hear from them about all of their concerns—not just the medical treatment, but how they were treated by staff.
- Call patients occasionally to conduct informal patient satisfaction surveys. A personal call means a lot.

See Chapter 4 for more information on "Getting Patient Feedback."

2

The Billing Department: The Importance of the Written Word

"My bill had a doctor's name on it, whom I had never met or heard of before. Also, I'm not a clinic patient, nor a "Rad" or "Path." You should be more careful and more accurate."

"It was my understanding that my insurance company would cover this. I was shocked to get a slew-o-bills. It turned out the plan was OK, but it was a costly mistake. I'm at a different hospital now."

These were actual comments on one hospital's customer survey regarding its bills and billing department. If you think the billing office doesn't have to concern itself with good customer relations because billers rarely (if ever) have direct dealings with patients—think again.

As mentioned in the introduction, increased deductibles and co-payments mean more patient involvement with business office personnel. Increased self-pay also means patients are paying closer attention to their hospital bills than ever before. That's why it's essential for billing statements to be accurate and easy to understand. Even though billers may never see or speak to a patient, they are directly involved in the public relations cycle.

This chapter will show you:

- How to establish a code of ethics.
- How to make your bills more reader friendly.
- How to fix any billing problem that is causing poor public relations.
- How to help patients understand their insurance.
- How to make sure you never breach patient confidentiality.

HOW TO ESTABLISH A CODE OF ETHICS

Fact: The billing department's performance can do a lot to help (or hurt) patient relations at your facility. This is why many billing offices have developed a "Biller's Code of Ethics" to establish a standard of excellence in billing practices.

Here are some ideas you could use when developing your Code of Ethics:

19. Create a pamphlet explaining your billing guidelines.

20. Send bills to both patients and insurance companies as soon as possible after service is rendered.

21. Keep late charges under tight control.

22. Inform patients at least every 30 days of the status of their outstanding debt.

23. Promptly acknowledge and correct patient complaints regarding billing errors.

24. Make calls to patients about billing problems only between 8 A.M. and 9 P.M. in the patients' time zones.

25. Complete all reasonable insurance billing and follow-up prior to referring the account to an outside collection agency.

HOW TO MAKE YOUR BILLS MORE READER FRIENDLY

How often have you heard patients complain that they don't understand their hospital bills? It's no secret—patients won't pay what they don't understand.

The Siegel & Gale Perplexity Poll asked 625 adults nationwide to rank common forms and documents according to their difficulty and reader satisfaction. Medical and dental insurance forms, college financial aid applications, and federal and state income tax forms were rated "unacceptable," according to the survey.

26. Review your bills for clarity and ease of understanding. If they look unclear to you, revise them.

Make bills simple and easy to comprehend. You want to encourage payment—not confuse the issue and delay payment.

In addition to checking for clarity,

27. Check for accuracy.

To avoid sending patients into shock the moment their bill arrives, it's important that the bill is correct and the patient understands the charges. It is vital for each bill to be clear and accurate. Be sure you understand the bills, or patients certainly won't.

Translate Terms

If providers don't take the time and effort to determine and communicate the patients' insurance benefits, self-pay portions of the bill have little chance of getting paid quickly. Most patients have no idea what their deductible or co-payments are, and many don't even know what the terms mean!

A recent nationwide survey of insured employees showed only 40 percent "completely" understood the term "coinsurance." Twenty-five percent understood it "somewhat;" 21 percent were "not sure;" and 13 percent had "never heard of it!"

To add fuel to the fire, day after day, the press, employers, insurance companies, and patient "advocates" are all attacking the same thing—your bill. As a result, many patients are convinced that rising health care costs are related to massive overcharging by the health care industry.

Fix the Bill

Faced with this situation, you need a new strategy. ***Here are a few suggestions:***

28. Explain the billing process to patients before or at the time of service. Have a procedure in place to tell your patients how billing works.

29. Clean up internally. A good preaudit program can help you find errors before the bill is sent out.

30. Train your staff on the telephones. When patients call with questions, make sure you're ready for them.

31. Review your statements/dunning notices. Send out communications your patients can understand.

Benefits of Bundle Billing

Rich Stewart, director of finance and reimbursement for the Metropolitan Chicago Health Care Council, Chicago, Illinois, notes the recent trend of more legible health care bills for the sake of patient relations. One of the ways health care facilities are creating user-friendly bills is by doing away with seven-page, 10,000 line-item bills. Facilities are going back to "bundle" pricing services, he says, that is, setting a specific rate for various services. The flat fee for open heart surgery, for example, would include everything—from surgeon and anesthetist fees to medication and the room charge. This eliminates the need to itemize every single item a patient needs, such as $12 for an aspirin.

Stewart compares bundle pricing to buying a car . . . "Your bill doesn't include a charge for windshield wipers," he says.

User-friendly bills are valuable, not only to the patients, but to the facility and the insurance companies as well, Stewart adds.

The Patient Benefits:

- "There are no surprises. They know they have to spend X amount. If they don't want to spend X amount, they go some place else."
- They don't have to go through pages of confusing line items and unfamiliar terms.

The Facility Benefits:

- There is less paper work and less time spent on paper work.
- Reduced customer complaints (for things such as the $12 aspirin).
- "Anything that helps the patient, helps the facility."

The Insurance Companies Benefit:

- They also have no surprises with the flat fee.
- It is easier to make cost comparisons among facilities.
- It makes their administrative life easier.

Another trend in health care bills is doing away with drug and medical supply symbols and getting back to using the English language, Stewart says.

When reviewing your own charging structure, Stewart recommends moving away from long, itemized bills and moving back to using the simplified language for clarity.

Benefits of Itemized Billing

There are benefits to itemizing bills, too. Some billing offices find the more that's spelled out in patients' bills, the fewer patient inquiries and complaints they get.

Marlene Snyder, a biller at Winter Park Home HealthCare in Winter Park, Florida, says their office bundles some services and itemizes others. "When I go to the grocery store, my receipt doesn't come out saying, dairy products = $54, meat products = $45," Synder says. "I receive an itemized account of the product and the price. And, of course, if I were to question a charge, I'd better be able to produce a proper accounting of my purchase with a detailed receipt."

Whether you choose bundling or itemizing the bill depends upon how your current method is working. If you bundle bills, for example, and they're triggering a slew of patient complaints and inquiries, consider itemizing instead.

32. Redesign bills, making them more simple, readable, and personalized.

Bruce Hallowell, director of patient accounts at the Morton Plant Hospital in Clearwater, Florida, completely redesigned the hospital's bills, making them more simple, readable, and personalized. It's more like a letter than an intimidating bill, says Hallowell. He calls it a "letter bill." It includes a narrative explanation of services patients receive.

And it's gotten some recognition in the industry. The Florida Hospital Association and the Healthcare Financial Management Administration, among others, printed news of Hallowell's letter bill in their newsletters. He's gotten close to 100 requests for a copy from patient accounts directors around the country.

A Better Bill

So, what is it about these letters that causes such a stir? According to Hallowell, the patient-friendly bills tell patients what's coming, including:

- a separate bill for physician fees
- more statements if the bill is not paid by a certain time

And it includes a customer service number for patients to call if they have questions or want to receive an itemized bill (for an example of Hallowell's letter bill, see Exhibit 2–1).

"Before, we were sending UB-92s to patients—the most confusing form in the world," says Hallowell, who adds that Florida law requires hospitals to send patients a copy of the bill. "What we did is take UB-92 revenue codes and translated exactly what they mean. (Patients) can go to the back (of the bill) and see, for example, exactly what laboratory services mean."

Putting It Together

The hospital's information technology (data processing) department took Hallowell's idea and transformed it into a program that works with the existing SSI patient accounting system.

How It Works: The program extracts the necessary billing information from the hospital's mainframe-based information system, converts it to letter form, and prints it out on the office's laser printer. This occurs at 4 A.M. each day, and automatically prompts the electronic billing system to begin editing claims.

Since implementing the letter bill, Hallowell says patient complaints have dropped from 1,500 per month in 1990 to 114 per month today.

(For more information about the letter bill, or to inquire about variations of the letter bill, call Bruce Hallowell at (813) 734-6420.)

Exhibit 2–1 Sample Letter Bill

Side 1

John A. Doe
705 N. Sylvan Dr.
Brandon, FL 33510

Dear Mr. Doe: Re: Patient Account Number 1800001256

Thank you for choosing Morton Plant Health Systems for your health care needs. You were a patient at our facility on January 26, 1996, through January 30, 1996, and the following summary of charges is supplied for your review:

Room and Board	**Days**	**Amount**
Semi-private	3	$1,500.00
ICU	1	$900.00
Ancillary Services		
Pharmacy		$2,000.00
IV Solutions		$149.10
Sterile Supply		$109.10
Laboratory Chemistry		$210.20
Laboratory Hematology		$124.20
Diagnostic Radiology		$3,190.80
Total Charges		**$8,183.40**

continues

Exhibit 2–1 *side 1,* continued

The amount due from you at this time is $8,183.40. You will continue to receive a statement until the amount owed by you has been paid in full. The statement will arrive in 15 to 30 days from receipt of this letter.

This summary of charges does not include most physician charges. Physicians, radiologists, pathologists, surgeons, anesthesiologists, consulting physicians, and others will bill you separately. If you have any questions regarding bills from your physician, please contact them directly.

If you would like to receive a detailed account of the above charges, please feel free to call (813) 555-7044 with your patient account number and one will be forwarded to you for your review. If you have any questions regarding your billing, please contact us at (813) 555-7044.

Side 2

Service	**Description**
Room and Board:	Routine services incurred associated with the nursing care.
Pharmacy:	Charges for medication produced, manufactured, packaged, controlled, assayed, dispensed, and distributed under the direction of licensed pharmacist.
IV Therapy:	Administration of intravenous solution by specially trained personnel to individuals requiring such treatment.
Laboratory:	Charges for the performance of diagnostic and routine clinical laboratory test.
Radiology Diagnostic:	Charges for the diagnostic radiology services provided for the examination and care of patients.
Nuclear Medicine:	Charges for procedures and tests performed by radioisotope laboratory utilizing radioactive materials as required for diagnosis and treatment of patients.
Operating Room:	Charges for services provided to patients by specially trained nursing personnel who provide assistance to physicians in the performance of surgical and related procedures during and immediately following surgery.
Anesthesia:	Charges for anesthesia services in the hospital.
Respiratory Care:	Charges for administration of oxygen and certain potent drugs through inhalation or positive pressure and other forms of rehabilitative therapy through measurement of inhaled and exhaled gases and analysis of blood and evaluation of the patient's ability to exchange oxygen and other gases.
Emergency Room:	Charges for emergency treatment to those ill and injured persons who require immediate, unscheduled medical or surgical care.
Labor/Delivery:	Charges for labor and delivery room services provided by specialized trained nursing personnel to patients, including prenatal care during labor, assistance during delivery, postnatal care during recovery, and minor gynecologic procedures if they are performed in the delivery suite.
EKG/ECG:	Charges for operating of specialized equipment to record electromotive variations in actions of the heart muscle on an electrocardiograph for diagnosis of heart ailments.
Medical Surgical:	Charges for supply items required for patient care.
Laboratory Pathology:	Charges for diagnostic and routine laboratory test in tissues and cultures.
Radiology Therapeutic:	Charges for therapeutic radiology services and chemotherapy are required for cure and treatment of patients.
CT Scan:	Charges for computed tomographic scans of the head and other parts of the body.
Blood Storage:	Charges for the storage and processing of whole blood.

continues

Exhibit 2–1 *side 2,* continued

Physical Therapy:	Charges for therapeutic exercises, massage, and utilization of effective properties of light, heat, cold, water, electricity, and assistive devices for diagnosis and rehabilitation of patients who have neuromuscular, orthopedic, and other disabilities.
Occupational Therapy:	Charges for teaching manual skills and independence in personal care to stimulate mental and emotional activity on part of patients.
Pulmonary Function:	Charges for tests that measure inhaled and exhaled gases and analysis of blood and for tests that evaluate the patient's ability to exchange oxygen and other gases.
Audiology:	Charges for the detection and management of communication handicaps centering in whole or in part of the hearing function.
MRI:	Charges for Magnetic Resonance Imaging of the brain and other parts of the body.
Observation Room:	Charges for minor procedures performed in the O/R or other room.
Psychiatric Services:	Charges for providing nursing care and employee, professional services for emotionally disturbed patients, including patients admitted for diagnosis and those for treatment.
Convenience Items:	Charges for items that are generally considered by the third party payers to be strictly convenience items and, as such, are not covered.

Important Information about Your Account

You are responsible for payment of this account regardless of insurance coverage. Even though an insurance claim is filed, you will receive a statement each month if your account has a balance due. This office cannot accept responsibility for collecting a settlement on a disputed claim. You are responsible for payment of your account. Delayed payment by insurance carrier is not a valid reason for delayed payment.

Source: Morton Plant Health System, Patient Accounts Department, Clearwater, Florida.

HOW TO FIX ANY BILLING PROBLEM THAT IS CAUSING POOR PUBLIC RELATIONS

Even though you don't usually come face-to-face with patients, you are in the service business. And, as shown in this chapter, billing without favorable public relations will lead to patient complaints and fewer dollars collected.

You can refer to Exhibit 2–2 to find quick billing remedies for what ails you.

National Billing Survey

Zimmerman & Associates LLC, a health care consulting firm in Hales Corners, Wisconsin, recently conducted a nationwide survey, asking approximately 1,200 patients in 60 hospitals what they thought of the billing and collection services they encountered in each hospital's business office. The survey revealed 4 out of 10 patients are unhappy with the hospital's billing and collection process. And, 6 percent of the patients were so disappointed with the billing and collection procedures that they would not return to the same facility for future care or recommend it to others. This means providers are losing more than 6 percent of their annual revenue for reasons that could be avoided.

Also, 30 percent of the respondents said they received no information during the billing process. Many patients were not satisfied with the ability of the billing representatives to understand their questions, and provide answers or solutions, and many complained about the speed with which an answer/solution was given. The unfriendliness of the representative was also a cause for discontent.

Take a look at Exhibit 2–3. It shows the survey responses. Answers in the "very dissatisfied" column, which ranged from 5 percent to 11 percent, includes patients who weren't just a bit

Exhibit 2–2 Quick Billing Remedies

The Problem	The Fix
1. Poor bill quality	a. Make sure bills are easy to read and understand. b. Concentrate on reducing late charges so patients aren't surprised with a bill two months after service.
2. Other departments lack knowledge of the billing department	a. Hold meetings with other departments to explain your objectives in detail. b. Write a regular feature in the organization's newsletter. c. Hold a billing office open house. d. Open communication lines with department heads. Invite them to staff meetings and make presentations at their meetings.
3. The public lacks knowledge of the billing department	a. Give reading material to patients during registration, stating the facility's billing and payment policies. b. Hold educational classes for the public. c. Conduct a public relations telephone survey after services are rendered. Review charges, bills, collection policies, etc.
4. Poor service by the billing staff	a. Train staff in technical areas and human relations. b. Upgrade job requirements. c. Update salaries and hire more qualified people. d. Give staff incentives and recognition for good performance in public relations. e. Concentrate on reducing stress in the office.

miffed by their experience, but were really angry about it, says Steve Chrapla, director of consulting at Zimmerman & Associates.

"If your hospital sees 100,000 people a year, 5 percent is 5,000 patients," says Chrapla. Hospitals should strive to keep the percentage down to just 1 percent or 2 percent, he says, allowing only for occasional miscommunications between biller and patient.

Your Own Patient Survey

Chrapla recommends providers:

33. Survey patients to find out where bills need improvement.

But, Chrapla says to be leery of the traps that often line an internal survey.

Two don'ts of a do-it-yourself survey are:

1. Don't ask for feedback then ignore it. This can be damaging to your business. Follow-through is critical.
2. Don't lay the blame on everyone else. Acknowledge the part the billing office plays in patient relations problems instead of merely pointing the finger at the physicians, the medical records department, etc.

What To Do

If you think your billing office is suffering in the area of patient relations, look at your process, advises Chrapla.

34. Track billing activity to determine where things are breaking down.

Exhibit 2–3 Survey Responses

	Very satisfied	Somewhat satisfied	Somewhat dissatisfied	Very dissatisfied
Billing and Collections				
Helpfulness of staff	70.6%	19.7%	4.5%	5%
Willingness of staff to listen to problems	71.59%	19%	3.7%	5.5%
Ability of staff to answer questions	68.9%	20.3%	4.4%	6.3%
Billing Assistance				
Ease of obtaining help	59%	26.6%	6.9%	7.4%
Courtesy of patient billing representative	66.7%	23.8%	4.4%	5%
Ability of representative to understand question/problems	61.7%	26.6%	5.8%	5.7%
Ability of representative to answer/solve questions/problems	58%	27.6%	6.4%	7.8%
Speed in obtaining answer to question/problem	56.9%	25.8%	8%	9%
Willingness of staff to arrange payment plans	52.7%	28.4%	7.7%	11%
Availability of suitable payment plans	52.9%	28.6%	7.5%	10.8%
The Bill				
Ease of understanding your bill	45.9%	33.8%	12.1%	8%
Accuracy and completeness of bill	45.9%	34.3%	10.2%	9.4%
Explanation of your insurance coverage	47.5%	30.6%	12.4%	9.3%

35. Build a flowchart of what should be happening and identify problems that can occur along the way.

Examine existing procedures for handling these problems. For example, bills sent to the wrong address leads to rebills and patient inquiries. What procedure do you have in place to get to the root of this problem and correct it?

Also, document how often problems occur and what is done to rectify them. This is key, says Chrapla. Don't just find out what the problems are. Fix them!

PR and Cash Flow

Good patient relations means steady cash flow. The two go hand-in-hand, says Peggy Zimmerman, executive vice president at Zimmerman & Associates. When patients run into problems with their bills, they're less likely to respond quickly or cooperate with payment, she says. The end result is delayed cash flow.

"Patients judge facilities on the quality of service they receive," Zimmerman says. "In the rapidly changing world of health care, the patient is becoming king. Those providers that do not give superior service will be forced out."

For a copy of the Zimmerman survey report, call (800) 525-0133.

Reducing Charge Errors

If a patient discovers incorrect charges—be prepared for an angry phone call. Eliminate charge errors, and you eliminate the stress of handling these calls.

The first step:

36. Reduce charge errors in your facility by understanding how and where they occur.

Armed with this information, billing managers can take steps to improve charge accuracy, thereby improving the accuracy of patient billing.

Case in point: Staff at Mary Hitchcock Memorial Hospital in Lebanon, New Hampshire, reduced charge errors from 3.5 percent of gross patient service revenue to .72 percent. According to the hospital's director of internal audit, Kenneth Spence, charge errors occur for several reasons.

Reasons for Errors

Depending on a hospital's sophistication and size, charges are recorded via a number of systems, including paper charge slips, bar codes, various computer systems, and physician requisitions, Spence says. Although systems vary, they all have at least one thing in common: A staff member submits the charge.

Here are some of the things that staff can do wrong:

- Enter the CPT procedure code incorrectly. For example, a patient comes in for a chest X-ray, but the X-ray technician transposes the numbers of the code so that a toe X-ray is charged.
- Fail to submit a charge. Using the example above, a chest X-ray may be performed and its interpretation may appear in the medical record, but no one enters the procedure charge. The reason for the oversight may be a simple one: The X-ray technician was distracted by another duty and simply forgot.
- Submit partial charges. Some radiology tests, such as angioplasty, involve several different components, including charges for the procedure, equipment, and supplies. A staff member may submit charges for the procedure and equipment, but not for the supplies.

Although many charge errors originate in ancillary departments, similar problems crop up in nursing units and operating rooms, as well.

In nursing units, for example, most medical-surgical supplies are on a cart central to the nursing unit, but a patient room may be at the end of the hall. Although the nurse takes the charge ticket with the supply item to the patient room, the imprinter is at the nursing station. As Spence says, nurses might get distracted many times before returning to the nursing station and, as a result, no supply charge is entered; consequently, the patient is undercharged. Overcharging can be a problem as well. This happens when the nurse takes a supply, charges it, but the patient doesn't use it.

In addition to human errors, the charge process itself can contain errors. Through no fault of their own, staff members may enter information on an outdated charge slip or computer software. Although the chargemaster includes the current charges and codes, the systems used in the ancillary departments or patient units might not have been updated.

Guidelines To Follow

Although there are a number of other possible sources for error, the point is clear: Reducing errors is a challenge.

You can face the challenge by adopting a few basic guidelines, including the following:

37. Make sure the information being used in the patient care areas includes the same information as the chargemaster.

38. Establish good communication with other hospital departments.

The key, Spence says, is information coordination. "People need to know who needs to know what and when."

39. Establish clear policies and procedures for charging and train new employees on established charge protocols.

When a charge changes, make sure all staff members involved know and understand the charge. Get involved when changes occur in the charge system. If a new system is implemented, make an effort to understand how it works. How are the different components (such as professional fees, technical components, and supplies) charged? Are they charged in bundles or as individual items? When appropriate, make efforts to simplify the system.

Important: Conduct training classes if your facility gets a new computer system. Without training, Spence says, "Getting a new system can cause disruption in the department and increase the work load if staff isn't familiar with it. There's no point in spending money on a new system without properly training the people who will use it daily."

40. Encourage billers to trust their instincts when it comes to charges that look unusual.

When they see a charge that looks "unusual," have them report it to their supervisor. For example, billers may see charges for numerous supplies, but no room charge.

41. Create a flowchart of the charging procedures used in various departments.

This will give you a pictorial concept of how things are supposed to happen and a better understanding of the many elements that make up the billing system. This will serve as a good training tool.

All of these steps will help you improve the charging process and reduce errors, but identifying the source of the errors and eliminating it is still the bottom line. Before you approach other departmental staff members about their role in errors made, do your homework and be prepared to confront them with hard data.

42. Review several months of charge errors and try to identify the source of the errors.

Sit down with department managers and explain the repercussions of charge errors and discuss ways to improve staff performance or the charge process. Continue your review and meet with managers again periodically.

Incoming Phone Calls

In some billing offices, billers are responsible for taking incoming phone calls. In one respect, this is good because billers are familiar with the account. On the other hand, this can also be disruptive to their work. The ideal situation is to create a separate customer service unit to handle incoming calls.

Whether billers in your office answer calls or not, you must:

43. Have a plan in place to make sure calls are answered swiftly, and patients' needs are taken care of quickly.

John Cornell, president of Quantum Resources, a patient account management and medical billing service bureau, says their office not only has a separate customer service unit to handle phone calls, it also has a plan in place to minimize calls and time spent on the calls.

Handling the Phones

The office has a balanced submission and mailing program to help accomplish this.

How it works: First, bills to patients are itemized. Cornell says detailed bills help minimize inquiries at their office. Second, bills are sent to patients in a timely manner. When primary payment from an insurance company comes in, billers don't wait until the end of the month to send bills to patients. Instead, bills are sent every Monday. This way, a steady stream of phone calls comes in every week, instead of a surge of phone calls once a month, Cornell says.

"Our office experiences essentially the same number of incoming calls each day as a result of our program. This enables us to maintain a customer service section with just two people," he says. "Their primary function is to answer all incoming calls and facilitate an appropriate response to the caller without depending on someone else. These people are carefully trained so they know how to respond and what to say."

"The customer service employees are required to finish their conversations with patients as quickly as possible—the goal being 30 to 60 seconds. If the caller requires more detailed information, customer service may transfer the call to a designated account manager or supervisor. But, less than 1 percent of patient calls are transferred outside the customer service area," Cornell says.

The customer service unit is also very organized in that it documents everything. "We require every call from a patient be logged into a computer file, no matter how trivial it may seem at the time," says Cornell.

The benefits of these practices at Quantum Resources are two-fold:

1. Patients are not transferred and "bounced around" in an effort to get assistance. They remain very cooperative as a result.
2. Account managers and billers are not bothered by the telephone. As a result, they maintain continuity of their efforts, which means fewer mistakes.

HOW TO HELP PATIENTS UNDERSTAND THEIR INSURANCE

In this day of managed care, patients are often in the dark on their insurance coverage and, consequently, come down on you, the provider, when things don't go right. Managed care is a whole new world to patients (and it might be for you, too). They don't always understand usual, customary, and reasonable denials, that they have a co-payment, or that they need referrals for specialty care. The latter is the number one cause for confusion.

It's not part of a biller's job description to explain patients' insurance coverage to them. Yet, to maintain good patient relations, you often must do so.

The need for referrals is particularly a problem at the office of Dr. Roy W. Jones, a respected and well-liked ENT, serving Denver, Colorado, since 1958. Suddenly, patients who had been coming to Dr. Jones for years were not able to come in without a referral, says Donna Jones, his wife and office administrator. All they can do is take the time to explain this change to patients, she says. They also chose to offer a 20 percent discount to patients whose insurance no longer covers visits to Dr. Jones, but who still wish to go to him.

"This office cares. It's not just the bottom line," says Donna Jones, who isn't happy with the changes brought about by managed care.

Tony Schirer, office manager at Capitol Hill Internal Medicine in Denver, Colorado, encounters another frustration with referrals. "Our biggest problem is they (patients) don't understand that they should have a referral before they see a specialist," says Schirer, who adds that internists can be the specialist or the primary care physician. "If they go to a dermatologist without telling us, they say after the fact that they need a referral, or worse, they'll wait until they get a bill. Then it's too late."

Another dilemma: A patient requests to see a specialist, but the internist can take care of the problem, so a referral is denied. "We say we can treat them here, and they don't understand why we can't give them a referral," Schirer says.

Patients who have had managed care for a period of time understand how it works, but new members of managed care plans haven't a clue, he says.

Solution: Staff is ready to help educate patients. To help them do this, they've designed a pamphlet explaining how to get a referral and when one is needed. The pamphlets are at the registration counter for people to take. If patients have further questions, staff will refer them to their company's human resource department or insurance company.

"Definitely, our number one problem is that they don't know about referrals," says Tish Severino, office manager at Irvine Medical Group Inc., a six-physician practice providing primary and specialist care in Irvine, California. "Patients get referred in and referred out. They're very confused about how it works," she says.

The entire staff is prepared to answer any questions patients might have, but they have one employee who specifically works with referrals. Most of the questions get funneled to her. The office also has a brochure that explains the rules and regulations of HMOs and PPOs.

Usual and Customary Denials

Not the number one cause for confusion, but definitely up there on the top of the list are usual, customary, and reasonable payment denials.

Patients are sometimes baffled by this, says Susan DeMartin, business administrator for the eight-physician Central Avenue Urgent Care in Montclair, California. Billers are in charge of taking these angry calls and smoothing things over, explaining what usual and customary means. Then they'll work with the patient, set up a payment plan, or write off the balance, if need be.

"You look at the incident and decide, is it worth making that person mad, or do you write off a couple of dollars?" says DeMartin. "But we usually don't have to. Most people know what they're responsible for."

In Review

As you can see, it often becomes necessary to educate patients about their managed care coverage. Consider doing the following in your office:

44. Keep copies of insurance policy handbooks in the office.

45. Develop handouts for each major insurance plan, outlining the five or 10 most common problems that occur under each and explain how each situation should be properly handled. Be sure to detail the patient's responsibility and what your practice will or will not do.

46. Design a pamphlet about referral procedures, if that's your number one problem.

47. Have one employee specifically in charge of handling managed care questions and referrals.

48. Update your policy handbooks and handouts with any changes that come your way.

49. Make sure everyone in the office understands how managed care works, especially the need for referrals.

The last thing you need is for a nurse or receptionist to send patients to a specialist without a referral. If that happens, you'll have a number of angry and bewildered customers.

HOW TO MAKE SURE YOU NEVER BREACH PATIENT CONFIDENTIALITY

Q: If you were in a traffic accident and a file of medical bills you had in the car flew onto the street, would you be liable for breaching patient confidentiality if someone picked them up and read them?

A: Yes, says Susan C. Manning, attorney and medical record administrator of Suby, Von Haden & Associates, S.C., certified public accountants of Madison, Wisconsin.

While this might seem far-fetched, it's merely an example to emphasize a point: Patient confidentiality is a serious matter. If you breach it, you can be fined, criminally charged, and even sent to prison. Furthermore, you risk the wrath of the angry patient whose privacy has been exploited and who is perfectly within his right to sue your health care facility for thousands of dollars. "Even if you're using a code, you are passing confidential information," Manning says. "A lot of people can figure out a code."

Another Danger Zone: Asking patients how they're doing with their medical problem in front of other people, or telling one person that "so-and-so" has cancer, then that person tells one more person, and so on and so on.

Bottom Line: Don't discuss patients' conditions casually.

Below are some of Manning's tips on how to maintain patient confidentiality.

50. Outline procedures for faxing and safeguards to verify that the receiver maintains patient confidentiality.

When faxing patient information to payers:

- Limit the use of the fax machine to urgent situations.
- Make sure fax machines are located in secure areas.
- Limit access to fax machine use.
- Identify the person responsible to monitor, remove, examine, seal, and route information.
- Outline procedures for faxing and safeguards to verify receipt. For example, you might want to fax a cover letter to the correct person first, then verify receipt with a phone call or by having the person fax back a reply. *Then*, fax the patient information and verify receipt again.
- Have procedures for misdirected transmissions. For example, immediately fax a letter using that same wrong fax number, urging the receiver to destroy the previously sent material. Then, make a note in the patient's chart.
- Follow patient confidentiality procedures.
- Release only to authorized receivers.
- Require consent when appropriate. About 30 percent to 40 percent of states require a signed patient consent form to bill and collect from a third-party payer, says Manning.
- Use a cover letter to include all pertinent data and consent.
- Maintain cover letter and consent in record (or copy).

51. Ask for the patient's name, address, telephone number, date of birth, and Social Security number when someone calls asking for a patient's medical and/or financial information.

Example: A patient calls her OB/GYN clinic and asks for what procedures she was billed. Take precautions before revealing this information.

The Best Practice: Ask the patient to make her request in writing. And always keep a signature on file. That way, when a written request comes in, you can check the signature against the one you have on file. If, by chance, the signature is forged, your legal protection is that you acted in "good faith," Manning says. In general, "good faith" is a nationwide protector against willful fraud and abuse.

Another Precautionary Idea: Ask for the patient's name, address, telephone number, date of birth, and Social Security number. If the patient stumbles or pauses when giving a birth date, that's a possible sign the person isn't who he or she says, states Manning.

Better idea: If you have time, ask the patient for the above information and say that you will call back with an answer. This way you can check the phone number against the one in your file. This is an added protection for you.

52. Train all staff on how to handle patient inquiries, and have each staff person sign a confidentiality form (Exhibit 2–4).

Mental Health, AIDS, and Drug and Alcohol Abuse Care

The sensitive nature of telephone inquiries is magnified when mental health, AIDS, and drug and alcohol abuse are concerned. In these cases, it's absolutely necessary to get the caller's request for information in writing.

Exhibit 2–4 Confidentiality Statement

I understand that it is my responsibility as an employee of __________________ to respect the rule of confidentiality. Under no circumstances are patients or their treatment to be discussed with nonclinical personnel. Any discussion of a patient and/or treatment is to be held in private areas so as not to be inadvertently overheard. No person outside of ______________ will have access to patient information, including any acknowledgement of the presence of the patient in the facility.

I understand that violation of this agreement will be grounds for immediate termination.

Employee signature: ________________________________

Date: ________________________________

Employee supervisor: ________________________________

Date: ________________________________

Note: If you work in a mental health or drug and alcohol abuse clinic and a person calls to find out if someone is a patient there, you cannot verify that information.

Workers' Compensation

Be careful! An employer might call up asking many questions about an employee who was injured on the job. Tell the caller you can't give out patient information. If the caller claims to be the patient, again, ask for their questions in writing, or ask for the name, address, telephone number, date of birth, and Social Security number, and listen for them to slip up.

Release Forms

Make sure new patients sign a release form if your state requires it (Exhibit 2–5). The release form authorizes the provider to bill the patient's insurance. Have the patient sign a new release form at least once a year.

Another idea: Include a place for a signature on the superbill. That way patients sign each time they're seen.

Minors

Releasing patient information to a parent of a 12-year-old child is a breach of privacy in some states. But in most cases, a parent or legal guardian is allowed to have access to billing or patient information for a child age 17 or younger.

Important: Know your statutes. Your state statute will spell out the details, such as what age is considered to be the legal adult age, 18 or 21, and what to do when the patient is a student at a college or university. You might want to develop a policy for dealing with sensitive procedures, such as pregnancy or AIDS testing of a minor.

Example policy: If you treat the patient without parental consent, then don't release information to the parent.

53. Know your state statutes regarding patient confidentiality.

To handle any of the above scenarios, refer to your state statutes. Study them; make them a part of your life, urges Manning.

To receive a copy of your state privacy statues, contact your state legislator's office, state medical records association, hospital association, or your state medical society.

Exhibit 2–5 Authorization for Release of Medical Information

Patient name: ______________________________ Date of birth: ____________
Last First Middle Initial

Street address: ______________________________

City: ______________________ State: __________ ZIP: __________

Authorize records released from:

Name: ______________________________

Street address: ______________________________

City: ______________________ State: __________ ZIP: __________

Records released to: ______________________________

Type or extent of information to be released (Check all applicable categories)

____ Medical history, examination reports
____ Operation reports
____ Treatment or tests
____ X-ray reports
____ Hospital records, including reports
____ Mental health records
____ Laboratory reports
____ Prescriptions
____ Consultations
____ HIV test results
____ Copies of all other reports
____ Alcohol, drug abuse reports

Purpose or need for release: ______________________________

This authorization will remain in effect until: ______________________________
This authorization will be effective for medical records generated to the date of signature.

I understand I may revoke this authorization at any time by providing my written revocation.

____

Signature of patient Date
(If signed by person other than patient, state relationship to patient)

Patient is: ❑ Minor ❑ Incompetent ❑ Deceased

Legal authority: ❑ Parent or legal guardian ❑ Next of kin of deceased

Source: This release form was designed by the legal council of the Wisconsin State Medical Society.

3

The Collection Department: The Essential Pleasant but Persistent Personality

Whether it's a fair or unfair assessment, the fact remains that collectors are seen as "bad guys" in the public's eye.

Patients see collectors as the people who are coming to take their hard-earned money away from them. Because of this, the collector may endure more stress and hostility than any other employee in a health care setting.

Given the bad rap collectors have inherited, it becomes especially hard to maintain favorable patient relations—hard but necessary.

Studies show only 4 percent of dissatisfied customers will complain. Ninety-six percent just walk away, and 91 percent will not return to you for repeat service.

Collectors must collect for the prosperity of the facility they serve, but they must maintain favorable patient relations, or these people will not return again to the facility for service.

It's been proven that the public responds much better to good public relations, or "goodwill" collection techniques. In other words, collections improve with good human relations and an emphasis on favorable public relations throughout your collection system.

Collectors are in a very difficult situation. But, if armed with proper customer service training, collectors will be seen by the public as professional, not rude.

How can you develop a professional, helpful, caring image? Essentially, there are two ways:

1. By offering various payment options to patients up-front, i.e., credit card payment, checks, and bank loans.
2. Making sure collectors' attitudes and collection letters are assertive, but courteous.

Important: While your job is to collect all that is owed, collecting with disregard for patient relations will only hurt collections in the long run. It's important to remind yourself of who patients are and to take the time to learn as much about each patient as you can. The more you know about them, the better your ability to collect from them. On the following page is a definition of who the patients really are. Make a copy to clip and post near your phone—just in case you need a quick reminder.

Who Are Patients?

- Patients are the most important people I come in contact with—even when they owe money.
- Patients are not dependent upon me. I'm dependent upon them for my livelihood.
- Patients are never an interruption of my work—they're the purpose of it.
- Patients are people I should never argue with. I will never succeed in winning an argument with a patient. I only hurt patient relations.
- Patients are not just names on files. They are people with feelings and emotions.

This chapter will go over how you can improve patient relations in the collection department by:

- Giving the patient payment choices—up-front.
- Collecting more with courteous, professional attitudes.

GIVE THE PATIENT PAYMENT CHOICES—UP-FRONT

This is the first tip for good customer relations in collections. If patients receive a bill two weeks or one month after service, they will be less inclined to pay. The urgency for health care is over, and their medical bill falls to the bottom of their bill pile. Collecting becomes difficult, or even impossible.

54. Collect at the time of service and offer patients an array of payment options.

This is good public relations, and you can avoid stressful collection attempts later on. You may hear objections to paying at the time of service. Here are some of the common ones and possible responses:

Patient: "I've never had to pay at the time of service before."
Collector: "Many patients like taking care of their balances up front so they don't have to worry about it later. That's why we're giving you the opportunity to pay now. Would you like to pay by cash, check, or credit card?"
or
Collector: "Paying now helps us avoid further billing costs. We're trying to do all we can to control health care costs for our patients. Now, how would you like to take care of the balance today?

Patient: "I thought my insurance paid for everything."
Collector: "I spoke with (name of insurance representative) at your insurance company. She verified that you have a deductible and a co-payment. You may want to call her later to clear up any concerns you may have. In the meantime, how would you like to pay for this today?
or
Collector: "We have verified your benefits with your insurance company, and I can assure you this is your responsibility. If we find out your insurance company has made an error, we will send you a refund immediately. Would you like to pay by cash, check, or credit card?"

Patient: "I didn't bring my checkbook."
Collector: "We also accept cash or credit cards."
or
Collector: "Do you have your credit cards with you? Or would you like to call home to get your credit card number?"

Patient: "My ex-spouse pays for all medical bills."
Collector: "No problem. I'll give you a receipt showing you've paid, and you can send it to your ex-spouse for reimbursement."
or
Collector: "If you put this on your credit card today, you can send the credit card bill to your ex to pay."

Patient: "I can't pay in full." *or* "I don't have the money."

Collector: "We accept all major credit cards for your convenience."

or

Collector: "When can you pay the balance in full?"

or

Collector: "That's fine. If you pay half today, we'll send a bill for the balance due in 30 days."

Examples of Front-End Collection Tips are:

55. Always start off by saying, "The charge is X dollars. Will that be check, cash, or credit card?"

56. Sell the patient on the importance of paying today. It's the best collection chance you have.

57. Always ask for the balance in full. Don't ask how much they can pay today.

58. If the patient cannot pay today, obtain a date the account will be paid in full. (Try not to go beyond 30 days.)

59. Develop urgency. Explain that the hospital or clinic does not carry accounts and request the account be paid today.

60. Persuade patients to pay their balance with a credit card.

Suggesting the use of a credit card is always an effective reply to the person who says he or she doesn't have the money or left his or her checkbook at home.

By persuading patients to pay their balance with a credit card, collectors receive payment in full immediately, and patients are able to pay off debts at their convenience. Both sides win, yet, only 6 percent of hospitals receive payment via credit card. And, as many as 90 percent of the nation's hospitals and 86 percent of group practices accept at least one major credit card! If more collectors would encourage the use of credit cards, collections would increase and angry patient/collector phone calls would decrease; thus, patient relations would improve.

Other advantages to the patient:

- Avoid collection agencies.
- Prevent adverse credit reporting by the hospital.
- Can make monthly payments to the credit card company.
- Maintain a good standing with the health care provider.

To increase use of credit cards, here are six suggestions:

1. **Post signs**—You need signs with credit card logos that are visible to the patient. Post them at entrances, the business office, cashier offices, and registration points.
2. **Put it on your statements**—All your statements should make it clear that credit cards are accepted. Also, make it very simple for patients to put their credit card information on the statement and send it back to you.
3. **Say it in your credit policy**—Make sure your credit policy points out that credit cards can be used instead of cash. The more options patients have to choose from, the more likely they are to pay in full.
4. **Sell credit cards constantly**—Admission clerks, financial counselors, cashiers, and customer service representatives, as well as collectors, must tell patients about credit cards, and must be trained to take charge payments.
5. **Convince them it's the right thing to do**—Many people will object to using a credit card because they want to save it for "fun" things

or they don't want to pay interest. Here are some motivators to convince them it's the right thing to do:

- *"I understand your concern. But, won't you feel better knowing you have paid the medical center that gave you excellent medical care?"*
- *"Paying this bill in full now means you won't have to worry about it anymore. You'll be able to make small, monthly payments on your credit card instead of paying us with cash now."*

6. **Overcome their excuses**—If they say, *"My credit card is to the limit,"* ask questions. Find out what the limit is, the current balance, how long they have had the card, and if they have a good credit history. It may be possible for them to extend their limit, or pay a portion of the bill with the credit card and set up payment arrangements for the balance.

PulseCards

The PulseCard credit card program not only gives patients another way to pay you in full, it also makes using other major credit cards at your facility easier.

How It Works: Patients who wish to pay their portion of the bill with the PulseCard simply fill out a quick application. Patients can mail in the application, or collectors can call it in and get a response in one hour. PulseCard statistics show approximately 45 percent of applications are approved.

If approved, funds will be deposited directly into the facility's existent checking account within 72 hours. You are charged a 5 percent fee for the transaction. (Most credit cards charge between 1.5 and 5 percent.) However, the unique twist is that your patient will be rebated 3 percent from PulseCard. This gives incentive to your patients to pay in full on their PulseCard.

Once you've received payment, your work is done because there's no recourse to you if the patient defaults. All billing and payments are handled by PulseCard. Patients are required to pay a minimum of $10 or 5 percent of the unpaid balance each month. The interest rate is quite low at 16.92 percent.

Patient BankCard Program

The Patient BankCard Program is another unique service offered by PulseCard. This program allows you to accept all the major credit cards at your office.

For a one-time set up fee, PulseCard will provide you with the ability to accept Visa, MasterCard, Discover, and PulseCard. The company provides you with all the supplies, forms, and information required to process credit card payments either electronically or manually.

As with PulseCard, all payments made on the other credit cards will be deposited directly into the facility's existing bank account. They also provide you with authorization forms that patients can sign giving you permission to charge future payments to any of the credit cards.

PulseCard is accepted at more than 3,000 health care providers nationwide. For more information about the program, call (913) 345-2522.

61. Consider a bank loan program.

Patients win with a bank loan program because they can pay off their balance with a payment plan that fits their financial budget. Minimum payments can generally be set as low as $50 a month. Patients are usually given a payment book to make payments easier.

The provider and the bank also win. The provider wins because the money owed is immediately paid in full. The bank wins because it has a new client paying interest on a loan.

Other Patient Benefits:

- The interest (usually between 12 percent and 15 percent) is usually much lower than most credit cards.
- Patients are able to consolidate all medical charges into one loan. This is convenient for the provider as well as the patient.

- Patients with a poor credit history have an opportunity to rebuild their credit rating. It's also a good way for young patients to establish a credit history.

62. Establish a financial counseling program.

If you took a survey of your patients, how many do you think would know what is covered and not covered by their insurance? Unfortunately, most patients know very little about their insurance. In fact, many think their insurance pays for everything—even when there's a large deductible or co-payment involved.

For this reason, it's a good customer relations practice to have extensive financial counseling programs in place to let patients know what their insurance pays and to provide financial counseling on the self-pay portions.

How To Handle Patients Who Pay You Paltry Sums

Despite your best efforts to collect payment in full from patients, sometimes they decide to make their own financial arrangements and send in only partial payments. Many patients (and some collectors) are under the false impression that as long as "something" is paid each month, the provider must accept it. Too often, collectors accept these terms.

When patients send partial payments without setting up a formal payment plan with the business office, it's important to correct the problem. Let patients know the balance must be paid in full unless formal payment arrangements are made. Acknowledge the patient's payment, but explain that payment in full was expected.

The sample letter in Exhibit 3–1 will help you persuade patients to either pay in full or establish a formal payment arrangement with your office.

COLLECTING MORE WITH COURTEOUS, PROFESSIONAL ATTITUDES

So you've offered patients a variety of convenient ways to pay their bills and financial counselors to help them with these payment plans. But it's inevitable. Collectors will still have to make the dreaded collection attempts on the back end. But, fear not! You can do so without losing grip of the favorable patient relations attempts on the front end. It's all a matter of treating others as you would want to be treated. With that healthy attitude in mind, you're on your way to successful collecting while maintaining good public relations.

Have you ever had a bill in collections? If so, how did you like to be treated? Did you pay the collector who harassed you and made you feel bad about not paying? Or did you pay the person who was understanding and helped you work through your financial hardship?

Most people will pay the understanding collector before they pay someone who beats them up verbally. And this is important to remember when you are the collector. Treating patients poorly will not only lead to complaints, it will hurt your collection totals.

63. Collect by Using the Golden Rule.

Collecting by the Golden Rule is a good path to take. *"Do unto others as you would have others do unto you."* In other words, treat patients who owe you money as you would want to be treated in the same situation. This is often easier said than done.

When you hear the same excuses for not paying over and over again, it's easy to start treating them less seriously than before. It's even fun to start making up sarcastic come-backs to some of the most overused excuses. When collectors get hardened to patients, they can run into trouble.

Exhibit 3–1 Sample letter

Mercy Medical Center

June 12, 1995

Charles Payshent
40 No Name Street
Anytown, MD 20878
Account #2390-33
Balance: $380

Dear Mr. Payshent:

Thank you for your recent payment of $50 toward your outstanding balance at Mercy Medical.

While we appreciate this partial payment, we must receive payment in full by July 12. After this time, if payment has not been received, the account will be considered delinquent.

If you are unable to pay your balance in full, we would like to work out a financial arrangement that would be acceptable to both of us. If you would like to discuss this further, please contact me directly at 555-5555 during regular business hours.

Sincerely,

Elizabeth Tyler
Financial Counselor

P.S. If you prefer, you can pay your balance using your Visa, Mastercard, or Discover card.

Here are some tips to make sure you're collecting by the Golden Rule:

1. **Be empathetic; not sympathetic.** Collecting by the Golden Rule doesn't mean you're going to fall for every excuse you hear and give up on payment. Rather, it means you will understand patients' situations but pursue reasonable payment options with the patient. Empathy means you understand how another person may feel. Sympathy means you feel sorry for them. You should strive for empathy with patients.
2. **Put yourself in the patient's place.** If you're having trouble getting patients to pay, get in the habit of putting yourself in their place—not so much to see how they feel—but more to find out what would motivate you to pay if you were in their situation. Looking at the collection call from this angle may give you some fresh ideas to motivate payment.
3. **Say, "I understand," during collection calls.** Sometimes just saying you understand (even if you really don't) might help you sound more empathetic. However, you must sound sincere. If patients sense insincerity in your voice, they might get angry with you. ***Try to avoid saying,*** *"I know how you feel."* This actually upsets patients. Many will retort, *"Don't tell me you know how I feel when you've*

*never been in my shoes." **It's better to say,** "I understand,"* because a person can understand a situation without ever being in the same situation.

Telephone Collections

For collectors, the tone of voice is just as important as what's being said. Does your telephone voice possess the following qualities?

64. Use a conversational tone.

You're just one person speaking to another. You're not a recorded message. Even when working from a script, it's important to keep your tone conversational. Always use simple and straightforward language.

65. Stay alert.

Your voice should have energy. Give the patient the impression you are wide awake and alert, even if you're not.

66. Use a pleasant tone of voice.

Don't whine. Your voice should be smooth and steady. Through your voice, try to communicate the message that you're a pleasant person. Never express anger or frustration in your voice.

67. Be distinct.

Use clear articulation and enunciate the words you speak. This is not as important in face-to face meetings as it is over the phone. The telephone tends to exaggerate poor enunciation.

68. Be expressive.

Try building a verbal image with your voice by varying your tone and rate.

69. Spend more than half of your time listening.

The way you listen to patients is just as important as how you speak to them. Good listening skills mark the difference between average and excellent collectors. Your ability to successfully collect is hurt when you're not listening. Try this technique. Tape record your side of a telephone conversation. Then, measure how much time you spent talking as a percent of the total collection call. This is a great way to find out if you're dominating the call, or if you're letting the patient talk enough while you listen.

70. Listen for ideas, not just facts.

Patients will offer a lot of excuses for not paying. You need to look at these excuses as "opportunities" not "objections." For example, a patient says, *"I can't pay my $100 payment this month because I have to pay $600 to my car insurance."* Rather than looking at this as an excuse not to pay, this is an opportunity to get a larger payment.

An insurance payment this large is probably for a six-month period. You could suggest to the patient: *"Did you know you could make monthly payments to your insurance company rather than paying all $600 at once? That means you'd have an extra $500 this month to clear up your past due medical bill while keeping your insurance current at the same time."*

71. Don't jump to conclusions.

Even though you've heard particular excuses 100 times, avoid anticipating what patients are about to say. Let them talk first. Act as if it's the first time you've heard it. Don't offer your opinion until you've heard what patients have to say.

72. Show interest.

Try to stay interested in what patients are saying even if it's boring or wordy. Don't let your mind wander because you could miss out on clues leading to payment. You can show patients you're interested by saying, *"I see,"* or *"I understand,"* during the conversations.

73. Never rush or interrupt.

Remember, it's rude to interrupt. If you're a rude collector, you're going to get rudeness back from the patient. Let patients talk at their own speed even though it may be frustrating.

74. Ask questions.

Asking questions helps clarify issues, clears up misunderstandings, and, more importantly, shows the patient you were paying attention. Most of your conversation should be made up of questions that encourage the patient to talk.

Remember: If you're asking questions the patient must answer, you'll be doing less of the talking.

75. Keep a positive attitude.

Remind yourself every patient is important enough to be listened to. Many times, all they want is to be heard. Once they've said their piece, they'll be happy to discuss payment. If you don't listen to them or pay attention, you run the risk the patient won't listen when you ask, *"When can I expect payment?"*

When the conversation heats up

Sometimes they scream. A few of them might even call you names or use abusive language. Whatever the case, dealing with irate patients is one part of the job no collector enjoys. Some irate patients have a valid complaint; others just need to blow off a little steam. But, there are always a few who intentionally try to evoke a reaction.

That's why it's important to:

76. Keep your cool when talking to hostile patients.

When on the phone with an abusive patient, it's not uncommon for a collector to simply hang up. This can be a huge mistake! In some cases, this is exactly what the patient is looking for. This type of person will complain about the doctors, nurses, the facility, and anything else that might lure the collector into an argument. If the debtor is successful, he or she might call back and ask to speak to a supervisor or president of the organization. At this point, he or she will explain how rude and abusive you were. The idea behind this strategy is to switch the focus from the debt to the "abusive behavior" of the collector. As a collector, you can't let an abusive patient get the best of you. Think, "good patient relations" at all times.

Here are some tips to keep in mind:

77. Be polite.

If the patient is trying to get a reaction, don't give one. Your best defense against a ranting and raving patient is to quietly listen to the complaint. The patient will find it difficult to continue yelling if you have a polite and helpful attitude.

78. Don't raise your voice.

This only makes an angry person yell louder. Instead, try to lower your voice. This will generally get them to quiet down, maybe just to hear what you're saying.

79. Avoid sarcasm.

Try to stay away from phrases such as, *"Gee, Mr. Jones, exactly how much coffee did you drink this morning?"* Not surprisingly, sarcasm will make the patient even more upset.

80. Don't hang up.

This response is very unprofessional and could work against you. As a collector, it's your job to turn an angry patient into a paying patient. Instead of hanging up on screamers, tell them, very politely, that you need to put them on hold for a moment. This will also give them a little time to cool off. Putting the patient on hold will give you some time to take a deep breath and gather your thoughts.

Warning: Don't leave patients "hanging" any longer than 30 seconds, or they'll be really steamed.

81. Don't take it personally.

Remember, screaming patients aren't mad at you.

82. Call back later.

If nothing else seems to work, tell the patient you would like to examine his or her account more thoroughly, and you will call back later. The patient is almost always in a better mood when you call back. Most of the time, the patient will apologize for his or her behavior.

Besides the urge to hang up on an irate patient, another natural reaction is to try to defend or try to prove the patient wrong. But it's better to agree than to argue with patients. How so? Here are some examples:

Complaint: "These charges are much too high."

Response: "I know. The cost of medical services is outrageous. I have quite a few bills myself. I wish there was something I could do to lower them for both of us."

or

Complaint: "My insurance should pay more."

Response: "I understand how you might feel your insurance should pay more. Why don't you give them a call so they can explain why they paid as they did? Then, you'll feel more comfortable paying the balance."

or

Complaint: "I had to wait two hours to be treated."

Response: "I can see why you're upset. I'd be upset, too. Why don't we get this bill cleared up as soon as possible so you can put it out of your mind?"

Here are five types of common debtors you encounter day to day and how you can handle each one:

- **The Know-It-All**—These are the people who know everything about everything (or so they think). They are very difficult to work with because our natural reaction is to try to prove them wrong. Trying to prove the patient wrong will only lead to uncooperativeness. Instead, keep calm and try to find some point you can both agree on. You may even want to compliment them on their vast knowledge, but watch the sarcasm.
- **The Arguer**—Arguers are sure someone else is wrong. They contradict and doubt everything you say. The best way to handle arguers is not to argue back. In fact, try agreeing instead. Also, deal with facts—they'll have less to argue about. Keep calm and focus on how to solve their problem.
- **The Nontalker**—Nontalkers don't want to discuss their personal affairs with an outsider. Try asking nontalkers simple, "no-risk" questions to try and draw them out. Also, explain the need for the questions you're asking. If you give them a good reason, they may open up to you.
- **The Talker**—The talker can be just as difficult as the nontalker. They want to tell you about everything—their illnesses, family life, their pets, etc. Try asking talkers close-ended questions requiring a simple, "yes" or "no" answer. Avoid the question, *"How are you today?"* You're asking for trouble. Remember, stick to the subject—payment.
- **The Demander**—Demanders think they are entitled to something they aren't. They want special treatment. The best thing to do is give them the special treatment they crave. If a

demander wants a payment arrangement, and your collection policy allows four months as the longest payment arrangement, try using this approach:

"Mr. Demander, our policy states payment in full is due in 30 days, but I understand your situation. Could you hold for just one moment while I check on something?" Put the debtor on hold for one minute. Then, say, *"Mr. Demander, I just checked with my supervisor, and because you are a valued patient, we have made a special exception for you. We'll allow you up to four monthly payments to clear your balance."*

How's that for customer service?

Tips To Improve Your Phone Skills

One of the best ways to improve "phone skills" is to evaluate collection calls from time to time.

Here are 10 questions to ask about a collection call.

1. How was the call handled? Was the collector enthusiastic? Friendly? Sincere? Was the call handled professionally?
2. Did the collector convey a level of confidence?
3. Was the collector courteous and polite to the debtor?
4. Did the collector listen to the debtor and not just recite a standard list of questions?
5. Did the collector use a pleasant and conversational tone of voice?
6. Was the debtor's name used throughout the conversation?
7. Did the collector offer solutions to the debtor's problems?
8. Was a payment agreement achieved? Did the debtor agree to send a check on a specific date or apply for a bank loan? Did the collector get a credit card number?
9. Did the collector repeat important information to ensure accuracy?
10. How well was the call closed?

Face-to-Face Collections

A key requirement for successful collections that's often overlooked is a professional image. Looking and acting professional is a skill that can easily be achieved once you recognize how it can improve your collection totals.

There are three main reasons for developing a professional collection image:

1. **Your patients' perception**—Anytime you have face-to-face contact with patients, they're making judgments based on your appearance and actions. If you don't make a positive, professional impression immediately, patients may not treat payment of your bill seriously.
2. **Your own perception**—What did you wear to your latest job interview? You probably wore something very professional that made you feel confident and mature. Your dress affects how you behave. If you are dressed sloppily or casually, you may have trouble collecting with confidence and authority. **Consider this scenario:** A patient comes in to discuss a bill wearing a professional business suit, and you happen to be wearing pants and a sweater. Who has the psychological advantage? Is your collection ability affected? You bet it is!
3. **Your boss's perception**—This may not be very important to everyone. But if you're looking for future promotion, your image will affect how far you go. You may not agree it's right, but the fact is, many less qualified people are promoted only because they displayed a positive, professional image. What can you do? There are certain characteristics working together to create your collection image. These can have either a positive or negative affect on the impression you make with others.

83. Wear clothing that enhances your ability to collect from patients.

The purpose of clothing is to enhance your ability to collect from patients. The more confidence, authority, and professionalism you portray, the better your ability to collect. Think of most people who deal with money—bankers, loan and mortgage officers, insurance brokers, etc. What do they usually wear? Why do you think they wear business suits? Wearing a business suit will help you send a message of importance and seriousness about paying a medical bill.

84. Maintain good posture.

Besides clothing, posture sends silent messages to other people—sometimes good, sometimes bad. You want to practice standing tall and walking confidently with strong strides. Use open gestures when working face-to-face with patients. Position your body facing theirs, not turned away. Also, look a patient directly in the eye when asking for money. This is a sign of confidence. If you look away or down at this critical collection point, you send a message you're nervous, or worse yet, you're lying. Strive to maintain eye contact with patients at least 80 percent of the time.

85. Use a firm handshake.

This is an important business custom often overlooked when collecting medical bills. You should introduce yourself, state your title or position, and offer a firm handshake before beginning your collection interview. Don't hesitate to offer your hand first. It will start your interview out positively and professionally.

86. Remember to smile a lot.

Unfortunately, your face speaks louder than your words when you're collecting. That's why you should always remember to smile. A smile goes a long way in establishing rapport with your patients. It will also smooth away some of the bad feelings that can occur when you ask for payment.

87. Be careful with your opening line.

The first words out of your mouth set the tone for the rest of the collection interview. Your opening line should be confident and positive.

88. Maintain a positive, professional attitude.

A positive, professional attitude supports all the other collection image factors. Without a positive attitude, all the other factors mean nothing. Take a good, hard look at your collection image. It could be hurting your collection totals and the public's perception of your facility. Take an honest look at yourself in the mirror and ask yourself, *"Would I pay me in full? Would I return to a facility after an encounter like this one?"*

In addition to the importance of your professional image in a collection interview, your surroundings have to be comfortable for the patient. First impressions can last a long time. That's why it's important for collection departments to project the right image to patients who stop by.

89. Place chairs for visitors in front of the collector's desk, never on the side of the desk.

Sitting on the side of a desk is not psychologically comfortable for the patient, and it's not as effective for the collector. A patient seated off to one side of your desk can infringe on your personal space and limit your perceived authority.

In addition to the placement of the chairs,

90. Make sure the area is attractive and neat.

Bookcases and credenzas are generally the only other pieces of furniture you should have in your office. If possible, keep filing cabinets somewhere other than in the office where you meet with patients. This will keep your office from looking too cluttered.

Above all, keep your office as neat as possible. If you need to have a lot of paperwork close at hand, try keeping most of it on top of a credenza or bookcase. A neat and clean desk is essential for projecting a positive image to the patient.

Collection Letters

Do you spend a lot of time smoothing the ruffled feathers of an irate patient who received one of your nasty or rude statements? If so, it could mean your collection notices are designed to make people mad rather than motivate payment.

In order to improve both your public relations and collections,

91. Review the wording and design of your statements to motivate—not irritate.

Patients often complain that health care bills and statements are difficult to understand, confusing, or do not provide enough information. When reviewing your patient correspondence, you may want to use a panel of your patients to give their ideas. Their input will help you design "patient friendly" statements and letters that will get you results.

92. Stay away from phrases such as "you must," "we expect," or "you are delinquent."

These types of phrases talk down to your patients and will cause them to get upset. Instead, use words and phrases that sell and motivate payment. Design them to show payment builds peace of mind and you want to help with payment options.

It's important to remind patients their account is past due, but never imply the patient is delinquent. Collection notices, just like collection calls, work better when they're used to motivate—not browbeat people. Use positive instead of negative phrases. For example, *"If payment is not received in 10 days, your account will be turned over to a collection agency."* This is actually a threat and stresses a negative consequence. For better results, write, *"We will not send your account to our collection agency as long as we receive payment within 10 days."* This statement shows the patient positive results for paying rather than the punishment for not paying.

Although collection letters and notices are not as effective as collection calls, they should still be designed for the best results possible—for the sake of collections and good public relations.

Your office should have standard letters and notices approved by administration that can be used in a variety of situations. Collectors shouldn't have to "wing it" when it comes to patient correspondence.

In addition, your statements, collection letters, and notices should be reviewed at least once a year to keep them up-to-date.

Here is a checklist you can use when reviewing your collection letters and notices:

93. Make sure collection letters are short and to the point.

Letters should be one page with only three to four short paragraphs and sentences with less than 30 words.

94. Eliminate words that may confuse your reader.

In order to sound important, it's easy to fill up collection letters with long, important sounding words. This will only alienate or confuse the reader. Always use shorter words that all patients will understand. For example, don't include "utilize" when "use" says the same thing. Watch for technical jargon that can confuse your reader.

95. Make sure your letter asks for payment in full.

96. Personalize the letter when possible.

Avoid "Dear patient." And have it signed by an individual, not the "collection department."

97. Include payment options such as credit card or bank financing in every letter.

98. Make sure your letter provides a way for patients to contact you (address and telephone number).

99. Include all pertinent information regarding the account, without overloading the statement with data.

100. Provide a return envelope to make it easy for the patient to send payment.

4

Getting Patient Feedback

As shown throughout this report, it's important to listen to patient complaints and not just apologize, but look deeper at what went wrong and fix it. As we've also mentioned, it can be helpful to come right out and ask patients, "How are we doing?" This chapter will show you how you can ask patients this question and use this information to establish better public relations.

PATIENT SURVEYS

To gather input from patients as to the impact of the patient accounting process on patient relations, consider conducting a survey.

Send surveys to patients of recently paid accounts and focus on their experience with hospital staff in the registration area and business office.

Rating scale:

Very poor:	1
Poor:	2
Fair:	3
Good:	4
Very good:	5

Sample Questions for Rating Registration Staff

1. Helpfulness of staff.
2. Professional appearance of staff.
3. Willingness of staff to listen to your questions or concerns.
4. Ability of staff to answer your questions or concerns.
5. Speed of the admission process.

Sample Questions for Rating Collection Staff

1. Helpfulness of staff.
2. Professional appearance of staff.
3. Willingness of staff to listen to your questions or concerns.
4. Ability of staff to answer your questions or concerns.

Sample Questions for Rating Billing Assistance

1. Ease of obtaining help with billing questions or problems.

2. Courtesy of patient billing representative.
3. Ability of representative to understand your questions or problems.
4. Ability of representative to answer or solve your questions or problems.
5. Speed in obtaining an answer or solution to your questions or problems.

Sample Questions for Rating the Patient Bill

1. Clarity of your bill.
2. Accuracy and completeness of your bill.
3. Explanation of your insurance or Medicare coverage.
4. Willingness of staff to arrange payment plan.
5. Availability of suitable payment plans.

Helpful Tips

- Send an equal number of surveys to inpatients, outpatients, and emergency room patients. Tally the results separately to help you see where you're going wrong.
- Make sure you include a comment section for patients to fill out.
- Add up the total responses and the average rating for each category.

POSTCARDS

Perhaps you don't have time to conduct a full-blown survey. Or, perhaps you want to keep the comments coming after you conduct a survey. Using postcards is a good way to follow up or keep up on public relations comments. Postcards can be used to gather good information about how patients view your facility.

A postcard survey is less costly than an extensive customer satisfaction questionnaire. Plus, patients are more likely to respond because postage is paid, and it won't take a lifetime to fill out.

Postcard surveys help to:

- Focus on specific areas of concern.
- Target a specific audience—new patients, emergency room patients, recent discharges, and outpatients.
- Reap quick tips to better please patients.

To get postcard surveys to patients, display them in a reception area. (Supply some pencils, too!) Or, mail them to patients within two weeks after service.

TESTING YOUR RESPONSE TO COMPLAINTS

Another good way to see how you're doing, in any department, is to adopt in-house patient complaint evaluation forms.

How it works: Each time a patient calls with a complaint, fill out a form indicating the complaint and what steps were taken to resolve it. This will prompt staff to pay close attention to patient relations, and see where policies and procedures might need improvement. And, if an unusual situation comes up, it can be discussed at the next staff meeting.

A form, such as the one in Exhibit 4–1, can be used to communicate what action was taken to resolve a complaint.

CONCLUSION

Hopefully this report has helped you see the necessity of good patient relations and how to attain it.

One final note: Good patient relations in the registration, billing, and collection departments all tie in together. If patients receive excellent service from the registration staff, but patient relations goes out the window on the back end, your facility

Exhibit 4–1 Patient Complaint Form

Patient name ______________________ Date of complaint ______________________

Account number ______________________ Balance ______________________

Complaint ____

____

____

Action taken to resolve complaint ____

____

____

Employee signature ______________________ Date ______________________

is in trouble. It's got to be like clock work. All three departments have to work together. Everyone in the entire facility has to work together—to provide excellent customer service and maintain favorable patient relations.

If nothing else, remember these few words of advice: Put the customer service policies and procedures in place; train, train, and cross-train your employees; then, revel in the improvements to your financial bottom line.

Notes

Notes

Notes

9 780834 209091

Printed in Dunstable, United Kingdom

91338350R00033